Retail

IT'S NOT

Rocket

Science

CATHY CARR

PAGE PUBLISHING
Conneaut Lake, PA

First originally published by Page Publishing 2024

ISBN 979-8-89157-980-4 (pbk)
ISBN 979-8-89157-998-9 (digital)

Printed in the United States of America

CONTENTS

HOOKED ON RETAIL

I have worked in retail for over twenty-five years and I love it. I absolutely love the vibrancy, the fast pace, the customers, the comradery—I even love most of the head offices that I have worked for. Obviously working with the public is not everyone's idea of a good time. There are certainly ups and downs, but as a whole, it can be a fun rewarding job. (Obviously I'm not talking in the monetary sense as it is the worst-paid job in the country.) It does get under your skin, and if you can afford to stay in retail, you may even get hooked like me.

So this book is a wee insight into my ideas and philosophies on not just surviving retail but being really good at it.

For starters, don't take it too seriously. You don't have to deal with life-and-death situations (you are not a doctor, social worker, or police). You are just selling a few T-shirts, pens, etc. Although in saying that you will not find anyone more competitive than me. I do like to win, so I love a challenge, whether it is beating the other stores in our chain or beating my own figures from last year.

Grow a thick skin. When you work with the public, you are exposed to the public. That means you will be exposed to the day they are having. For example, they may be sad, happy, grieving, angry, disappointed, frustrated, etc., or a combination of the above. It doesn't mean you have to absorb any of this. But it does mean you have to listen to it. Put up an invisible barrier ten centimeters from your face, and decide that's where it all stops. You don't have to let it in. People may need to verbalize it to you, especially if they are complaining about a faulty product you have sold them, but you personally don't need to absorb it.

You don't need to take on their emotion. What you do need to do is stay calm, let them have their say, and then calmly deal with any situation. Don't absorb their anger, frustration, etc.

Our auntie has a grandchild who recently started working in retail. She put something on Facebook about "I am going to make them say hello to me if it kills me." Hilarious! If anyone has worked in retail, they know exactly what she is talking about. Rude people, which is another thing you don't need to absorb. Some people are just downright rude. So what! Get over it. Again, that ten-centimeter barrier. That's about them, not us.

JUST SAY "HELLO"

"Just Say 'Hello'" was the second choice for the title of this book. Seriously, you can't underestimate the value of acknowledging the presence of a customer. After all, they are the ones indirectly paying your wages/salary. As people get older, I hear them say they feel like they become invisible. But in actual fact, older people are often the ones with the big disposable income. They no longer have dependent children at home, their kids will be out of university, and their mortgages are paid off, so their disposable income is all theirs.

When I worked in a jeans store, I was really busy one morning. I had two customers in the fitting room that I was looking after, plus another two ladies browsing. Another woman walked in, and I said "Hi, how are you?" as I walked past to get something for one of the other customers. I didn't even wait for an answer—just smiled and kept going. I then went and rang something on the till. This lady came over and thanked me for my awesome service! Seriously! I couldn't believe it. All I had done was say hello. She said, "I have just been in to two other stores and was totally ignored. The girls were behind the counter and just chatting." Hard to believe that this still happens in retail today, but there you go.

Years ago, I went to a sales conference, and one of the speakers was saying that the average age of the people buying a prominent-brand motorcycle was sixty-three. They didn't want you to know that, but that was their statistics at the time.

As retailers, we need to be aware of that demographic and give our staff the awareness and appreciation of the older generation and what they mean to our business.

BE A GOOD GUARDIAN
MAKE A DIFFERENCE

love working for chain stores and have worked for quite a few different ones over the years. The thing about them is the ones I have worked for have been around for quite a few years and will continue to be around long after I have left them. So I always just consider myself a guardian of whichever store I am working for. In saying that, I ask myself every day, "Am I being a good guardian? Am I earning my keep today?"

I have been lucky enough to have been sent on projects for some companies I have worked for, doing fashion shows, expos, setting up new stores or just minding new stores for their first week of opening, around the country. I always ask myself, "Have I made a difference? Has it been worth it to the company to spend the money flying me around the country, putting me up in nice hotels and paying for nice dinners for me?"

Example, I did a roadshow for one of our stores out of town, and we didn't have a lot of customers coming to our booth. So I took our catalogues and stood at the door and smiled and said hello to everyone and gave them our catalogue and told them about the fashion show we were holding in-store the next day as they entered the expo. I thought surely someone was going to come and ask me not to do this soon, but they never did. I think everyone thought I was the official greeter, and as it turned out, I was. This is one example where I felt I earned my way. I feel proud that I made a difference.

We can all make a difference (or not) each and every day. It doesn't just have to be on a project. It is also every day in your store. If your team know that they can make a difference every day, surely they will be more motivated to do so.

I have this example I give to all my new team members. I tell them if we sell one stapler for $20, we have paid $10 to get it into store, then we have $10 profit. But then out of that $10 comes staff wages, rent, electricity, insurance, etc. So then if we add on a $20 hole punch to that same customer, then we get the $10 for free as those costs have already been covered. Obviously, that isn't the case as the costs are dissolved into two items. But if you explain it to a six-teen-year-old student, they understand the principle behind it. Even the most naive sixteen-year-old can understand that. This gives them a clear, concise understanding of the importance of adding on.

Another great example I have used in a bookstore I worked at. We did 250 transactions on a slow day and 900-plus transactions on each day in December. So let's say 400 transactions on average per day. So if we add on one $1 stamp to every customer, that equates to $400 per day. Which is then $2,800 per week, which is then $145,600 per year. Now the company I worked for had 67 stores, so this equated to $9,755,200.

Now obviously we won't add a $1 stamp to every customer. But for some of the customers we will be adding a $45 book or a $10 tee. The above example just highlights what an add-on can do and how important an add-on is. Even one as small as a $1 stamp is still important. It equates to millions and millions of dollars. (Again, that naive sixteen-year-old gets this.)

This is a really simple way of looking at it. Keep it simple.

LEADERSHIP

When you manage a store, you are the leader. Too often I see managers that don't realize that they are the leaders in their business and it is their responsibility (or even in their ability) to set the culture of their work environment. Not just for their benefit, but for that of the whole team.

If you are a positive, fun, fair, can-do-attitude leader, then that will be the culture in your store. If you are a negative Moaning Myrtle, then that will be the culture in your store. So managers need to realize that setting the culture of your store is (1) possible and (2) very important.

Always treat your company with respect, and even if you don't agree with some of their decisions, as manager, you are paid to implement those decisions, so introduce them in a positive light. I have heard staff say, "What has the company ever done for me?" Well, even if they don't give you bonuses or have made you feel valued, they have funded your life for the last whatever number of years you have worked for them—paid your mortgage or rent, funded your kids' education, and put food on your table. So even if you feel overlooked by your company, you still owe them your existence. Don't lose sight of the value in that.

If I am asked to list what my biggest strength as a manager is, I will say that it is that I am calm. I don't just jump on people's bandwagons. If they have a gripe or complaint about something or someone, I don't just automatically agree with them. I always take time to think about the issue and think how I really feel about it. Just because they feel that way about something, or have an opinion about something, it doesn't mean that it's right.

EMOTIONAL OWNERSHIP

One of the best things you can do as a manger is to give your team emotional ownership of the success of the business. I can't stress enough the importance of emotional ownership. This is everything. It motivates you, gives your work purpose, and makes you work harder to strive for success.

There are many facets to giving your team emotional ownership. They need to feel that they can make a difference and be proud of the difference they make.

I often brainstorm ideas with my team. As manager, you don't always have to come up with the ideas, but for goodness' sake, don't take credit for someone else's ideas. If I am implementing a great idea that isn't my own, I will always say, "Johnny suggested _______." A good manager can come up with lots of ideas themselves. They don't need to steal the credit belonging to someone else. We have all had a boss that takes credit for other people's ideas, and let's be honest, they just make themselves look bad.

Training is another way to give them emotional ownership. You need to teach them to think commercially astute so that they can make good decisions for the business. And once you have done that you need to let them make decisions. You then need to give them a safe environment to make these decisions because, even though sometimes they may not make a great decision, they will learn from these, and so long as they are learning from these decisions, they will go on to make good ones, with your guidance in a positive, fair manner.

HIRING YOUR TEAM

Every chain store I have worked for has a set hiring process to follow, which is good. However, I know in the first minute of meeting a candidate whether or not I want them on the team. That first minute is crucial as this is what your customer gets every day. Do they look openly at you? Good eye contact, comfortable facing you? Are they well presented? Are they positive and happy to be there? Obviously, they may be nervous, but their ability to be comfortable in a retail environment will be obvious at this first meeting. Are they a people person?

The next stage is the interview. Here they think they need to convince you that they are good enough. But funnily enough, the interview just tells me if I can bear to spend eight hours a day with them.

Basically I just need to find out if they are positive, nice, kind. Do they have empathy, and most of all are they fun? If they are fun for me and the team to work with, they will be fun for our customers to shop with.

I know that to even get an interview these days, you have to have all this experience, but basically if your candidate has all the attributes listed above, then they will be a fantastic retailer. Or at least as good a retail as you are able to train them up to be. A quote from a past area manager, "After six months, you will have the team member you deserve to have because you will have made them what they are." referring to training.

So experience doesn't matter as they will be as good as you make them. The things that make them a great retailer are the attributes listed above. We can't teach them those. They either have them or they don't.

Don't always look for someone exactly like you. Great teams are made up of individuals with different strengths, so you don't need to hire another you—you are already working there. To have a strong team, you need someone with different strengths from you. Keep that in mind. Your team doesn't need to be made up of clones of you.

TRAINING

One of the key attributes to a successful team is training. Our teams are not telepathic. It will be great if they are. But they are not. So your training needs be done in a clear, concise, calm, nonthreatening environment.

As I start a new team members training, I always ask how they like to learn. Do they like to write everything down? Do they like to do something five or even ten times? Or do they like a little bit of both? Don't stand at the till and show them how everything is done. Put them on the till and talk them through how to do everything. It's that left-brain, right-brain thing. Hand, eye, brain. When they have done it themselves, it cements in their brain much faster than if they have stood there and watched you. I make sure I train them in their optimum mode of learning. Rather than just expect them to learn the way I like to learn. That way they will learn in a comfortable way and learn so much quicker.

I once had a boss teach me the way she liked to learn and then sit there and huff and puff and roll her eyes because I wasn't taking it in fast enough. As opposed to another area manager that said I was the quickest person to pick everything up that she had ever trained. Seriously, that is result of a good trainer (and a not-good trainer). Which performance would you choose for your new team member?

A forty-year-old who has been in retail for fifteen years is obviously going to need less training than a sixteen-year-old school leaver who has never done retail before. You need to get both of them from point A to B. However, this will be a different training experience you need to give them. It doesn't mean one is better than the other. It just means you need to train them differently. And that means that you have to be the skilled trainer to get them both to point B. One may take a week, and one may take a month. But that doesn't matter—it is about you getting them to point B. So often I have heard managers say, "Jonny is useless." But actually it just tells me that they are useless at training.

You need to be specific with your training and delegation. What do you want them to do. How you want it done. And what time frame do you expect it to be done in. You also need to give them the big picture—the reason we need this done. This is crucial and one of the most frequently overlooked aspects. Don't underestimate your team having the big picture. Once again, this impacts on the emotional ownership and therefore their commitment to the success of the task.

A quote from a previous area manager, "The only thing worse than training someone and have them leave is not training them and have them stay." Love it.

LEARNING TO LET GO

When I moved to a big-turnover store, I had to learn to let go of the reigns sometimes. This may feel uncomfortable and certainly took a lot of growth on my part. I managed to do this successfully by the aspects discussed in the previous chapters. I had to delegate effectively. I had to train (or delegate that training) well enough that the team member can be trusted to do a great job in my absence. Whether that be doing the task or them delegating the task effectively.

Don't micromanage. Give them the skills to think for themselves. Give them tools to make good decisions and the confidence to make those decisions. Then take a step back and let them use those tools and skills. Create a positive learning environment. This is one where they know if they make a mistake, you won't belittle them or make them feel useless. They can then move on from that mistake and learn from it.

When I train someone, I never ask, "Do you understand that?" I always say, "Have I explained that okay?" It puts the responsibility back to me. That way, they don't feel dumb if they have to say they don't understand. They realize I haven't explained it in a way that is good for them.

If they feel they are having a positive impact, it will make them enjoy the job and feel pride in their work. They may make some bad decisions, but so long as they learn from these, okay. I always say if my team member is doing something wrong, then it is my fault because I haven't trained them well enough or given them the tools or skills to be competent.

They will feel valued, and they will be valuable to you as a strong team member.

DELEGATION

When I started at the bookstore, there were seven different departments. The store I had come from prior, I could have run single-handed. Obviously, this was not going to be the case in the bookstore, so I had to learn effective delegation, and fast.

I am a great believer in getting the team to think for themselves. Obviously within reason, as we don't want rogues. An area manager used to say to me, "It's not a democracy. The final decision is yours." And he is right. The manager does have the final say. However, I believe we should give the team the guidelines and boundaries to make their own decisions.

You need to upskill your team to the same level you are at. I know some managers feel threatened to do this, but I just feel proud that I have developed my team—and don't forget about succession. You won't be around forever, so you need to set the business up well to continue strongly without you.

An example of a way I did this (and you can adapt this to suit your business needs) is when I had a student start with us. She worked the late night. I trained her in things she could do to help out other team members in their departments when she wasn't needed at the till. I physically took her through the tasks, and we wrote a to-do list to cross out as she finished each task. Then the next week, I got her to write her own to-do list and cross out each task she managed to finish. I then asked her to leave her list on my desk for when I came in the next morning. She did a great job at managing her own time/tasks, and after two weeks, I said she no longer needed to leave me the list as I knew she was competent. She now thought for herself and took lots of pressure off the department holders by topping up and tidying their areas while working the late night.

This only works if we are all on the same page—remember emotional ownership—make them realize they matter and they have the power to make a difference. They start to feel proud of what they are doing and what they are contributing to the team. Remember that $9.7 million in Be A Good Guardian. That's what I am talking about!

WORKING FOR/WITH A BULLY

What can I say? Presumably if you have been in the work-force for any amount of time, you will have come across a bully. We have all been there.

The only positive I have taken from working with bullies is that it has made me a better manager. They highlighted what I don't want to be as a boss. And made me realize that being a manager should not be about my own power but about empowering other people. Even though there are legal avenues to go down to address bullies, many of us just don't bother.

I have found bullies are usually domineering personalities, and that seems to stem from their own insecurities. They need to feel like they are in control because they are so scared of not being seen as the boss or in a position of power. They think no one is listening to them, and let's face it, we aren't. We are pretty much just waiting for them to finish their rant or telling us off. And then of course we then have no emotional ownership of the success of the business, because who wants to do good for them? Not me.

So the only other thing I want to say about bullies is don't be one! When you put us down or make us look bad in front of our coworkers, you are actually making yourself look worse than us.

What you say about/to people tells me more about you than what you are saying about that person.

The few times I have wanted to rant and rave at someone, I have walked away until I have calmed down, because let's face it, we are all only human, and we do sometimes lose our temper, but I would never lose my self-respect enough to yell at someone or belittle them.

Don't get me wrong. I am not a pushover. I set high standards, and my team has to meet them. If they are not meeting them, then first of all, I look at the training.

A great example of this is when I had a school student working our late night, a shift that my 2IC always ran. The 2IC came to me and said, "I can't get any work out of [let's just say Johnny]. He's useless." Now this Johnny actually worked really well for me. So alarm bells were ringing because she obviously wasn't giving him clear, concise direction on each shift.

So the problem was me. I hadn't given my 2IC the skill of delegating. That was a great lesson for me, and I learnt a lot because of it.

STANDARDS/HOUSEKEEPING

Many managers have a bugbear. I had an area manager who was obsessed with sticky tape left in windows, whether it was on the glass, racks, walls, or floor.

Mine is the window display. Well, one of them. But it is my biggest.

I often walk past a window display, and there might be dust motes or a poster askew or even half down. And these things do happen as we are all busy and we can become store blind. However, my bugbear is when it stays like that for days on end. There is an easy way to keep your store window, and store, to the high standard you need it to be: checklists. My team every morning have to look at the window and check that it is fine. For some reason, midges come in our window to die. Even though they don't come into the store, we often find thirty of them on the floor in the window in the morning. And not every morning, just some mornings. That's why it is important to do your checklist each morning. In the bookstore, we would have recovery time. At 4:00 p.m. each day, everyone had to stop what they were doing and walk around and straighten the store. It's so easy to get caught up in how busy you are and all the tasks, you need to make it a habit of all your team to keep the standards high. You need to plan for it. It doesn't just happen.

YOU ARE THE FACE OF YOUR BRAND

If you are working in retail right now, then you are representing your brand. Ask yourself, "Am I representing it well?" On the shop floor, you are the face of your brand. Are you representing it in the way that you should be? Do you have a smile on your face? Are you friendly and approachable for customers? Are you clean, groomed, and not tired or hungover? Do you look the part? Are you wearing their brand if you work in fashion, and if you are, are you wearing it in a way that would give you credibility to style customers in it? If you work in a jeans shop, by all means wear jeans, but wear them like a Kardashian, not a Bogan.

This is where you can make a difference. Be a great representative of your brand. Make the brand proud and lucky to have you as their team member. Respect the company you work for, and be a great guardian.

MERCHANDISING

Most companies spend a lot of time, money, and energy getting their merchandising right. This is their face of the brand. It is important to adhere to their directives. However, often you will not have all product required for a window or interior display and will have to improvise.

I have talked about being commercially astute, and this is definitely one of those times where profit should play a part in your decision making.

Example, there is an outdoor concert scheduled for your town, and it is raining today. Shall I put some clearance $10 tees on the front two-way rack? No, I will not. I will put our $169 raincoats up there because I might sell three, giving us an extra $507 in the till, whereas I will have to sell fifty-seven tees to get that same money. Commercially astute. Think about profit. There will be times when those $10 clearance tees are appropriate, but due to local factors, that time is not today.

Be cleaver about the placement of your product. If 10 percent of your sales come from socks, don't commit 40 percent of your floor space to socks. Or am I only selling 10 percent sales in socks because I only have 10 percent of floor space committed to these? Try committing more, but analyze it and make changes if not working. Be aware of where your sales are coming from. You may be a chain store, but your store will have different strengths from that same chain in another town. Get to know your own market—what works and what doesn't. But don't get stuck on these. Things that may have not worked last summer may work this summer with different attitudes changing in your community. Try different things, but always analyze the effect they have on sales.

Another example is when we had a blue, red, and white window display with jeans and tees. We had a gorgeous red raincoat come into store, so I added it to the window and sold nine of them before any other stores had sold any.

Be creative and think outside the square. How can I make a difference? Each time you make a decision, you should be thinking, "How will this affect profit? Which is the best option for generating profit?" Little things add up to big things. Chip away at it.

THE CHANGING FACE OF RETAIL

Retail has had a significant change over the last ten years due to the Internet. Not only are our customers now shopping online, but they are making a lot of choices online even if they are purchasing in your store.

The Internet doesn't necessarily have to be the baddie. In fact, the Internet can be a huge advantage to us with our loyalty database. We just have to be prepared to get on board, and for a store to do that successfully or to their full advantage, the staff need to be committed to this. And like so many aspects of training your staff, they will need the big picture.

Explain to your staff we can send our message (whether it be about a sale, event, etc.) to three hundred customers or thirty thousand customers. To get their commitment, managers need to be committed themselves and seen to be committed.

Example, our company sends out stats of how many sales are linked to VIPs on our database. So as a manager, I talk about this. I sing our teams praises when we feature highly. They know I look at this and will discuss if they are not doing this. I tell them that we are doing the customers a disservice if we don't link their names as they accumulate points for vouchers.

THE THING ABOUT RETAIL

One of the things I love about retail is that when people come into your store, you just see them. You see who they really are. We are not our car, our house, our job, or our income. We are what's in our heart and soul. And when customers come in, we get to see them, the real them, because you have no idea what their job is or what car they drive or how much their house is worth.

It may be a small glimpse that we get, but an accurate one.

Sometimes we think the world is full of doom and gloom and dangerous people because this is what we see on the news each day—violence, murder, robberies—and we perceive this as our world. Even though those things do exist in our world, they are such a small part of it. Seeing it on TV every night makes you think that is what human nature is. But it isn't. Human nature is the teenage lad who finds a wallet in the back of your store full of cards and seventy dollars cash and hands it in at the counter. It is the lady that finds twenty dollars on the floor and brings it up to the counter. In this instance, I took her name and phone number and said if no one claimed it that day, I would phone her as I was not going to take it to the police station as such a small amount. So when the lady came to pick up her unclaimed twenty-dollar note, she brought us a box of chocolates, which probably cost fifteen dollars. That is the real human nature that exists out there. And if you are lucky enough to work in retail, it is these people that you will experience each day. Maybe not every single day, but many days.

Sometimes we have things going on in our lives that can cause stress or unhappiness. But when you walk into your store, you can chose to leave that part of your lives at the door. Work can be somewhere you come to that you don't have to focus any anything negative going on in your personal life for the next eight hours, or however long your shift is. You can choose work to be your happy place. Shelve all the bad stuff and just focus on enjoying your customers and team and choose to have a great day.

Once you are able to do this, you will find that you are now making everyone around you have fun and a great day too. Not just your team, but your customers also.

When I have a new team member, I love to tell them about the reading book my son brought home for his homework when he was five. In the book, his mother gave him a smile when he left for school, and he gave that smile to the bus driver, who then gave it to another child, who gave it to the caretaker at school, who then gave it to his teacher, who then gave it to him when he walked in the classroom. It is important to realize as a retailer, you may be the only positive person your customer sees today. You can be a small snapshot of happiness in their lives. You can make a difference to them right here right now. Even with just a smile.

So if you are working in retail, enjoy!

ABOUT THE AUTHOR

Having had a career in retail management for over twenty-five years, Cathy shares some of her insights on how to run a successful, motivated, positive team. One where the customers enjoy to shop and where the team enjoy to work. She manages two retail stores, so knows all the ins, outs, highs, and lows of the day-to-day running of a retail operation.

Cathy lives in New Zealand with her husband. They have three sons and five grandchildren, plus a huge, wonderful extended family.

www.ingramcontent.com/pod-product-compliance
Lightning Source LLC
Chambersburg PA
CBHW031640170726
47990CB00018B/1575